A Critique on Person in Kierkegaard

A Critique on Person in Kierkegaard

Xavier Pfokrehe Mao

CONCEPT PUBLISHING COMPANY PVT. LTD.
NEW DELHI-110059

ISBN-13: 978-93-86682-65-9

First Published 2020

Published and Printed by

Concept Since 1974

Concept Publishing Company Pvt. Ltd.
A/15-16, Commercial Block, Mohan Garden,
New Delhi-110059 (INDIA)
T : 91 11 25351460, 91 11 25351794
E : publishing@conceptpub.com, *W* : www.conceptpub.com

Cataloging in Publication Data--Courtesy: D.K. Agencies (P) Ltd. <docinfo@dkagencies.com>

Mao, Xavier Pfokrehe, 1962- **author.**
A critique on person in Kierkegaard / Xavier Pfokrehe Mao.
pages cm
Includes bibliographical references.
ISBN 9789386682659

1. Kierkegaard, Søren, 1813-1855. 2. Individuation (Philosophy) 3. Christian philosophy. I. Title.

LCC B4378.P47M36 2019 | DDC 198.9 2323

This book is
dedicated to
My Father A. Loli Mao
and
My Mother A. Matiro Mao

Foreword

The small monograph relating to Kierkegaard submitted by Xavier P. Mao is excellently well written essay. Usually, the Existentialist Philosophy that too of Kierkegaard appears difficult and unintelligible to most of the Indian students of Philosophy. Further, to students of Analytical Philosophy, existentialism appears to be a bundle of contradiction and inconsistency. Mao has taken all possible care to remove this type of misunderstanding.

Kierkegaard uses the concept of individual to explain existential problems, but Mao replaces it by the concept of person for the sake of convenience as he admits it. When the individual is highly concretized it becomes a person. In this sense, a person is a conglomerate of hopes, aspirations, ambitions, anxieties, pain, passion, sufferings and so on. Even it can contain highly contradictory features like faith and distrust, belief and disbelief and so on. This might appear as a contradictory position, but the existentialist like Kierkegaard save the situation by arguing that it is the individual who knows best what is to be done. In this sense Kierkegaard accords place of primacy to existence over essence. In a very important sense existential problems could be solved by resorting to sentiments, passions, emotions and such like. The existentialist particularly Kierkegaard while emphasizing sentiments and passions, faith and belief talks of total surrender. This religious dimension brings Kierkegaard very close to Christianity and Mao has very clearly and carefully made this point. To add to it, this aspect of existentialism brings it very close not only to Christianity, but also to *Bhakti* Movement that developed and flourished in India during the medieval period.

Mao argues out in detail that Kierkegaard's way of understanding man is an attack on conceptual and categorial mode. To understand man in terms of fixed categories and thus, to define him as a rational animal is to speak the half truth. The Hegelian way of understanding man and society in terms of fixed categories and concepts is to miss the vital point. Mao has argued out and has defended Kierkegaard's position in a very pointed and very convincing manner.

The ideas of absurd and absurdity, contradiction, suffering, loneliness, sin and salvation are crucial to understanding Kierkegaard. On the surface, these ideas are likely to create confusion, but Mao has taken special care to explain these basic and vital concepts. Man is not a fixed and finished product; he keeps on changing and growing. This aspect of man has been emphasized and explained by Kierkegaard. While growing man changes and this appears contradictory and confusing. But, this is a fact that while growing man changes and this constant change and growth make an individual unique. In this sense every man is unique and if one lives and conducts oneself in accordance with one's passion, sentiment and feeling one can be said to be leading an authentic life. Authentic life is unique. Kierkegaard terms this subjective life of man as inward movement of spirit.

Mao anticipates criticism against Kierkegaard's view of man and society. Subjectivism, solipsism, amorality and moral relativism are common charges against existentialism in general and Kierkegaard in particular. Mao is inclined to side with such critics, but with sufficient reasons. It may be mentioned in this connection that Philosophy not only aims at presenting an alternative thought structure; sometimes, it aims at presenting alternative way of life. Seen in this light, the existentialist view of passion, inward movement of spirit and such others come very close to the life of an *Avadhut* (renunciate) and Radha and other Gopis consumed with devotion and surcharged with love described in Vaishnava tradition in India.

N. MALLA

Retd.

Professor of Philosophy and
Dean, School of Humanities and Education,
North-Eastern Hill University, Shillong, Meghalaya

Preface

The philosophical inquiry for Sore Kierkegaard is not the construction of systems or to build grand metaphysical theories in trying to explain everything. It is also not what the Anglo-American philosophers emphasize as the linguistic, logical and conceptual analysis. For him philosophy is the expression and the profound Socratic examination of the single individual as the knight of faith. It is precisely for this reason he composed his epitaph for himself as "That individual". But, I have replaced person for the individual for the better understanding of the readers as that is the common contemporary usage. His writing is in a sense inimical to neat, logical and systematic clarity of expression. His existentialist philosophy of choice is at the edge of a precipice risk of being submerged into the romantic philosophy of feeling due to his emphasis on the passionate inwardization. According to him, the ultimate choice is criterionless. The replacement of inwardness by an ecclesiastical worldliness is like living the life of a mass man and not the singled out person of the crowd or the herd. By living the high degree of self-awareness in passion and deep inwardness as a knight of faith in Christian God one can successfully distance oneself from the social identity. To be a true Christian for him an individual ought to subordinate one's reason to the authority of a revelation that is given in paradoxical form in the person of the incarnation of Jesus Christ which I find extremely difficult to accept and strongly disagree with his philosophy. It seems to me here Kierkegaard by smuggling in the concept of the Leap of Faith has tacitly accepted the Christian metaphysical presupposition that a caring, loving, omnipotent and omniscient God exists. As an agnostic it seems to me such presupposition is against the very spirit of Socratic self-examination.

Xavier Pfokrehe Mao

Acknowledgements

I feel it appropriate to express my affectionate appreciation to Prof. Margaret Chatterjee, Dr. Ved Prakash Gaur, Prof. S.R. Bhatt, and Prof. Ram Chandra Gandhi for the valuable suggestions and guidance. I would also like to express my gratitude to Prof K.J. Shah for critically discussing Kierkegaard's Philosophy with me.

I am very grateful to Mr. Wanpli Majow for the necessary typing. I am thankful to Dr. Prasenjit Biswas for the arrangement of index.

Xavier Pfokrehe Mao

Contents

1
The Concept of the Subject and How and Why Kierkegaard Moves Away from It?

To begin with I would like to make it clear that the term 'Person' is not used by Kierkegaard. I replaced 'Person' for Kierkegaard's 'individual' for convenience. By way of analysing the concept of 'person' negatively, 'person' is not an essence or substance or abstract entity, which underlines various phenomenal activities. 'Person' is not the subject or cognizer, since the subject is essentially an epistemological term, i.e. it has a cognitive connation. On the other hand, 'person' is an ontological term, i.e. human being as a totality.

The concept of 'person' emerges clearly in the following contrasting manner as:

- Person *vis-à-vis* subject,
- Person *vis-à-vis* thing,
- Person *vis-à-vis* system, and
- Person *vis-à-vis* crowd.

For Kierkegaard, the person is a living creature and moreover, living has an inner drama. In other words, life is an internalized drama. It is an inner drama in the sense that Kierkegaard was all the time in a state of encounter with God and his conscience within himself. Unlike other living beings, the person has self-consciousness. Self-consciousness is the mark of the human being. We are all the time moving between the polarity of 'is' and 'is not', 'yes' and 'no', 'interested' and 'not interested'. The person is an ethical religious being, the single one. The person is not the crowd, but he/she is singled out of the crowd. He/she is set apart from collectivity. Human is not a species since each human being is different and unique. This uniqueness is highlighted in the religious life and not in the aesthetic or ethical life.

The person is neither the soul nor the mind. The person is the 'I' Kant talks of as an end. The person is finite, incomplete and distant from the infinite.

Positively, becoming subjective is the task proposed to every human being as his highest task which lasts throughout life. Kierkegaard's key thought was that his own age, because of the great increase of knowledge, people had forgotten what it means to exist and what inwardness signifies. Further in his view Hegel's conflation of speculative philosophy and Christianity revealed the same neglect of human existence. If human had forgotten what it means to exist religiously, they had doubtless also forgotten what it means to exist as human beings, this was his sincere belief.

Kierkegaard argues that it is easier to indulge in abstract thought than to exist in the true sense, i.e. inwardly. It is like an irony that existing is ordinarily regarded as no very complex matter, much less an art, since we all exist. But, really to exist, so as to saturate one's existence with consciousness, and yet have a sense of eternity far removed that is truly difficult.

In this difficult task, the person is in process of becoming the experiencing individual. Kierkegaard is against any static conception of the person, to live is to strive and for this reason Kierkegaard constantly talks about fragments, and crisis, questions like 'what should I do' and 'where should I go'. Socrates said, "The unexamined life is not worth living." This idea of self-examination Kierkegaard emphasized. The human being is very vulnerable. In other words, we are always vulnerable. Unlike human beings, things do not have an inner life. A person is one who is all the time aware of threat. According to Kierkegaard, some threats are from outside and some are from the inside. So, the person is under fire all the time.

Some of the threats are endless speculation, abstraction, collective life, mechanics, institutions and conventions. These crush the person, the existing individual. The key to this reality is one's own experience, and this brings in responsibility. Therefore, he is constantly relating the person to ultimate matters or concerns. Ultimate concern here is the destiny of man. This is the reason why he is all the time drawing a distinction between life and thought.

Kierkegaard's distinction between life and thought is the entire sharper when he reacts strongly against system-building, logic and Hegel's absolutism. For Hegel, the absolute is more than the individual. The individual is just a part of the absolute and the reconciliation is through dialectical movement. But for Kierkegaard, the individual as an existential being is in space and time concretely and discretely. It is the person who makes an existential choice and this choice is not ordinary choice but one that affects the entire life. Hegel's rational system, being formal, is cut off from concrete living reality. Logic cannot tell us about life. Human existence, on the other hand, is ambiguous and complex, therefore, to say that it is ambiguous is to say that logical system will automatically exclude the reference to existence.

Thus, existence and system cannot be thought together. "System and finality correspond to one another, but existence is precisely the opposite of finality. It may be seen, from a purely abstract point of view, that system and existence are incapable of being thought; because in order to think existence at all systematic thought must think it as abrogated, and hence as not existing. Existence separates and holds the various moments of existence discretely apart; the systematic thought consists of finality which brings them together."[1] System is generality and abstraction, system and finality go together as mentioned above. Therefore, existence cannot really be captured by concepts. "The systematic idea is the identity of subject and object; the unity of thought and being, existence, on the other hand, is their separation."[2] For us thinking and being have a gap. But for Hegel thought and being are identical. Since Hegel has a monistic system. Being is one. And nature is the objectification of thought.

But says Kierkegaard, existence is contingent for us. Existence is open, incomplete and fragmentary. The existing individual is perpetually striving. There is intense involvement and engagement.

For Kierkegaard existentiality is to do with the peculiarity of being human. Here peculiarity means the uniqueness of every existing individual. The human being is for life and living. He is not a thought like a triangle is a concept or 2 + 2 = 4 is a concept. The human being is in space and his existence is temporal. That is to say he has an inner existence. To have inner existence means to have hope and fear. Hope and fear give the key to his existentiality. Man is aware of the conflict between duty and inclinations. Human existence is ambiguous, i.e. we are and we are not. Human experience is replete with mixed character. Ambiguity arises in action too. Human existence is open to various possibilities. Only the past has finality. The present and future are open ended. This persistent striving of the individual represents the consciousness of being human. For this he goes on to say that man is not primarily a knower or cognizer, but he is a doer. Doing here means living. He is not an activist like Blondal or the pragmatists. And in doing, faith is the light. Faith is a kind of madness. Without risk, there is no faith and where there is calculation, there is no risk. Risk means may be or may not be. In this we have to minimize reason, because paradoxical situations are beyond reason. If I am capable of grasping God objectively, I do not believe. But, precisely because I cannot do this, I must believe. Subjectively is unique to each individual. There cannot be adjudication about this. Faith tells us that eternity has come into time, which is absurd. Another absurdity is that we can use our freedom to choose. Life consists of a series of choices, but since one is free, tomorrow one can choose in a totally different manner from what one chooses today. Life is considered as a series of events, and one has played one's part. Therefore, there is a sense of absurdity about decision, since one keeps on changing. Thus, one is just floating in uncertainty and in time.

The animal has instinctive programming and patterns, but human beings have many possibilities and options. It is in the light of this that Kierkegaard seriously objects to such definitions as:

'Man is a rational animal; 'Man is a child of god'; 'Man has *avidya'* (ignorance) etc. For Kierkegaard and even other existentialists, to give a definition is to delimit. Thus, Kierkegaard's shift broke away from the objective world to the subjective world.

The way of objective reflection makes the subject accidental, and thereby transforms existence into something indifferent, something vanishing. Cut off from inwardness the objective way of reflection leads to objective truth. And when the subject and his deep inwardness become indifferent, the truth also becomes indifferent. This indifference is precisely what objective validity is. In sharp contrast to this, all decisiveness is rooted in subjectivity, in the deepest core of the inwardness of the existing individual.

Christianity is essence in spirit. Spirit means inwardness and inwardness is subjectivity. Subjectivity is essentially passion. Passion at its maximum is an infinite personal, passionate interest in one's eternal happiness, i.e. direct encounter with God. Here God means the personal benevolent Christian God. If subjectivity is eliminated and passion eliminated from subjectivity, and the infinite interest eliminated from passion, then there is no decision at all and there is no living either.

For Kierkegaard it is only by way of faith that we can attain 'inwardness' or truth. And on individual subject realizes the true meaning of his inwardness or subjectivity, in the supreme subjectivity of the divine being through faith. For Kierkegaard God is the Supreme Being. The individual man in his plenitude cannot be exhausted merely in the concept of man. He is essentially a being never to be disclosed to anybody other than himself. He cannot be conceptualized nor can he be an object to himself. The person as a self-disclosing being is not a logical concept but a concrete being, or reality. But, its concreteness is not like that of an object or a thing but is that of a striving being.

The subject moves away from the object and from itself as a cognizer to realize its full being and destiny. But, this moving away is not like the Pharisee in the temple who proudly found satisfaction in seeing the publican. It is like that of the publican who humbly and absolutely saw no one, not even the Pharisee, but remained with eyes cast down and turned deeply inwards. He was in truth kneeling down directly before God in sin. To give one more illustration, the subject's moving away from unreality is like that of a great sinner and at the same time a great saint, Mary Magdalene who wiped the feet of Jesus with her tears and dried them with her hair. It is such an act done in sin, done in the place of subjectivity, which is more lonesome than the desert of loneliness, in the place which is more lonesome than the most unfrequented path that one encounters God—it is in such subjectivity and face to face with God's holiness that the cry spontaneously issues of itself. His cry would call upon someone else to help where there is literally no one else, but God. It is the supreme subjectivity, which is experienced only in inwardness through faith that Kierkegaard is talking about, when he argues that truth is subjectivity.

Note

1. *Concluding Unscientific Postscript* by Soren Kierkegaard, Translated by David F. Swenson & Walter Lowrie, Princeton University Press, 1974, pp. 107, 112.

2
What is It That Individuates the Human Being?

For Kierkegaard, passion is the individuating factor of the human being. Passion here means suffering. All existential problems are passionate problems. Suffering again is through faith. Faith is not this or that thing, but a whole way of living. Such a whole way of living is not matter of what one eats or wears, but what place eating and wearing occupy in one's life. Each human being is unique and is an open-ended being. Further, particularity can never be grasped by a network of concepts.

Kierkegaard emphasizes the importance of 'faith' as a faculty, which allows the 'individual' to be in his innermost cores of consciousness, that is, the sphere of subjectivity. Thus, faith alone can enable us to have an inward experience of God, or faith is the highest passion. From this it follows, therefore, that the direct encounter with god brings about the realization of our true distinct individuation as a human being in contrast with animals or other beings. It also further implies that we are necessarily related to the infinite subject. Also our direct encounter with the eternal being of God establishes us as inter-related beings. It follows, therefore, that it is only as an Ethico-religious personality that an existing individual realizes God and at the same time comprehends the significance of inter-subjectivity. But, here it should be made clear that Kierkegaard has a limited meaning of inter-subjectivity, i.e. between God and the ethical individual alone. Unlike Gabriel Marcel, for Kierkegaard life does not shine in inter-subjectivity between the different ethical individuals. It is for this reason that he is sometimes branded as a solipsist. As argued in the preceding pages, reflection, Kierkegaard points out, may help us formulate many a view of life, but it cannot absolutely supply the essentially religious and eternal view of life. "The way of objective reflection makes the subject accidental, and thereby transforms existence into something indifferent, something vanishing. Away from the subject the objective way of reflection leads to the objective truth and while the subject and his subjectivity become indifferent, the truth also becomes indifferent and this is precisely its objective validity, for all interest, like all decisiveness, is rooted in subjectivity."[1] Thus reflection or reason can in no way make inroads into the region of faith. Kierkegaard, therefore, tells us that leaping into the depths, one learns to help oneself and ultimately realizes one's true being.

Thus to exist means choosing one's own true self. Existence is something to be won by choice. Kierkegaard, therefore, suggests to us that the subject should be infinitely concerned about himself and this involved the process of becoming and striving. According to Kierkegaard's understanding, Christianity is intensified passion. Therefore, an Ethico-religious life is nothing comfortable or cozy but makes us full of concern. This passion is the very opposite of meditation, meditation in the sense of not churning, but being still and calm. For Kierkegaard probably calmness never came. He was always in a storm and turbulence. Life for him is all the time churning up passions in fear, remorse and trembling. The individual ought to be worked up, engaged, concerned and worried all through life. It is the hallmark of the individuating factor of the human being to bring about such passion. The ethical individual should be aware of the sense of sin, aware of the finiteness and contingency of human existence. Such a view of life in Kierkegaard perhaps had been shaped by his childhood experience, the Christian conception of original sin and the romantic age he belonged to.

The reflective penetration of existential suffering gives to guilt-consciousness. The existing individual continues the regressive penetration of him by reflecting upon the existential state of suffering and brings to consciousness a still deeper and more concrete level of existence. It is only in suffering that the individual becomes conscious of a contradiction between himself and his absolute telos.

According to Kierkegaard human is totally guilty. But, he says that this is not to be determined empirically. The concept of guilt, understood as a totality, belongs essentially to the sphere of religion. Even repentance is not a direct movement towards God. But, it is an inward movement towards oneself through which the individual completely understands the nature of himself. Through repentance, the ethical person binds together the whole movement of self-choosing, because the individual's freedom in its greatest concreteness is disclosed and chosen. Kierkegaard refers sin as a mode of consciousness.

Resignation contains the deepest consciousness of suffering. And suffering contains the still deeper consciousness of guilt. Guilt again contains the deeper consciousness of one's whole state of being in inwardness as a mode of self-consciousness, making way for the act of repentance. The next level of consciousness is the consciousness of sin. But sin-consciousness, according to Kierkegaard, is not a reflected level of consciousness. It cannot be understood by human reason from the preceding level of existence. Self-consciousness, on the contrary, depends upon the historical revelation of God in time. To allow one self-consciousness to be informed by such revelation required an act of faith.

According to Kierkegaard, Christ is essentially the model, and consequently every existing individual should be like him. Christ being the Deity in time, unlike the existing individual, possesses the ideal perfectly, and therefore, does the noblest thing freely. But the deity in time is not simply the ideal man in whom we find our humanity through imitation, as he is for Kant, but he is also the one who forgives sin.

The model of ideality is also the savior and atoner. Kierkegaard asserts that the existing individual must have the courage to believe existentially in the ideal. Belief also required the much more radical existential appropriation of oneself as sinful. Belief also requires the acceptance of oneself as need of divine forgiveness, if the ethical requirement is to be fulfilled.

Kierkegaard emphasizes that to exist in the existence medium of sin is very much a matter of faith. Even the notion of forgiveness of sin is equally a matter of faith. Further, it is through belief in the forgiveness of sin that the existing individual becomes spirit; to believe this forgiveness of one's sin is the decisive whereby a human being becomes spirit, he/she who does not believe this is not spirit.

Kierkegaard further argues that sin is human's destruction. Only the rust of sin can consume the soul or eternally destroy it. In order that one's soul may not be destroyed, one has to undergo suffering. Just as gold is purified in the fire, so is the soul in suffering. Gold loses in the fire all its base elements, i.e. by losing, gold gains in the fire. So, it is with all temporal suffering which in itself appears to be impotent. But, if the sufferer allows eternity to have a say, it takes away the impure elements. In other words it becomes endowed with purity.

In this suffering, faith is the only blessed assurance which is found in fear and trembling. Faith seen merely from the human side appears to be sheer fear and trembling. When faith is seen from the heavenly side, one sees sin its only the bright reflection of blessedness.

This is best illustrated by the woman that was a sinner. She sits weeping at Jesus' feet. Initially, the environment was calculated in such a manner to remind her frightfully and languishingly of herself. But she has altogether forgotten herself, forgotten the environment with all that is disturbing in it. Her own inward world is perfectly quiet. In weeping, there is also this blessing, i.e. forgetfulness.

In deep inwardness, terror is discovered and with the discovery of terror the need for prayer is discovered. The spontaneous cry arises; "God be merciful to me a sinner" this cry is so sincere that now the existing individual is in perfect communion with God. And this is the perfect individuation of the human being away from the objective world and the subject as a cognizer.

Note

1. *Concluding Unscientific Postscript* by Soren Kierkegaard. Translated by David F. Swenson & Walter Lowrie, Princeton University Press, 1974, p. 173.

3
The Destiny of the Person

In this last chapter it is appropriate to raise the question "what we are born to?" In response to this according to Kierkegaard, the person is a forward oriented creature, that is to say he moves in time, never complete, always on the way. There is nothing like a 'human nature' or 'essence' in human, from beforehand. He/she is like a blank sheet, a *tabula rasa*. He/she never comes in the world as a finished product, as ready-made, as well-defined. But, he defines himself by living in the course of this life in the world. It is I only by living, thinking and acting that human defines his/her nature and forms what is called his/her essence, that which he/she is and will be.

Human is engaged in existing. Human existence is very ambiguous, that is, it is and is not. Human existence in the past has finality. But the present is very fluid and the future is still open. Therefore, whenever there is openness there is no system, because a system is fixed and totality. Human existence is fragmentary, that is to say in time. To be in time means that human is aware of his/her existence and experiences time. We are future-oriented beings; this is what it is to exist. Thus, "man is a rational animal" does not tell us anything significant about human, according to Kierkegaard. To objectify the human being is to direct him/her. Because anything which is in time is never systematic and real.

The existing individual is constantly in the process of becoming. He/she constantly reproduces this existential situation in his thoughts and translates all his thinking in terms of process. This incessant becoming gives rise to the uncertainty of the earthly life where everything is uncertain.

The task of becoming subjective is presumed to be the highest task and this is the case for every human being. And its corresponding highest reward is the eternal happiness as it exists only for those who are subjective. Furthermore, it is assumed that the task of becoming subjective provides a human being with enough to do to occupy him/her for his/her whole life. In this way, it is not the ethical zealous individual, but only the restless one who manages to get through with life before life gets through with him/her.

It is only momentarily that the ethical individual asked to realize existentially a variety of the infinite, the infinite which transcends existence. This variety is supposed to be realized in the moment of passion. "The paradoxical religiousness defines the distinction absolutely by accentuating paradoxically what it is to exist. For as the eternal came into the world at a moment of time, existing individual does not in the course of time come into relation with the eternal and think about it, but in time it comes into relation with the eternal in time; so that the relation is within time, and this relationship conflicts equally with the thinking, whether one reflects upon the individual or upon the Deity."[2] Modern philosophy and science have tried each and everything in the effort to help the individual to transcend himself objectively, which is an attempt which is totally impossible. Such an attempt is bound to failure, because modern philosophy holds passion in contempt. Yet for Kierkegaard, passion is the culmination of existence for an existing individual. And we are all of us existing individuals.

By being in passion and inwardness the existing individual becomes aware of the significance of the religion and of the big leap. Consciousness impels one to higher resign or surrender ultimately. Resignation is a higher understanding of the act of choice by which human relates himself/herself to his/her self.

Kierkegaard accepted the Socratic principle of self-knowledge. But this superficial comparison cannot be stretched too far because for Socrates "know thyself" is not a religious maxim at all, whereas Kierkegaard for talking is from the religious point of view. God does not reveal Himself in the objective world but rather in the innermost subjectivity.

It is in inwardness that human finds his/her God-relationship and thereby raises serious philosophical questions concerning the ontology of God. If God is one's innermost subjectivity, how is God to be conceived in relation to the self-structure? Kierkegaard would agree that to raise such a question is to bring reflection and reason into the sphere of faith. But, for him it is through faith and in faith alone that Christian hope, expectation, salvation and eschatology, shape the destiny of the person.

Notes

1. *Concluding Unscientific Postscript* by Soren Kierkegaard, Translated by David F. Swenson & Walter Lowrie, Princeton University Press, 1974, pp. 505-506.
2. *Ibid.*

4
Conclusion

Person and Persons

Kierkegaard's understanding of the concept of the person is guided by his concept of the nature of God. And further, his concept of the nature of God as a person is an insight he received through the incarnation of Christ, eternity entered into time. The life of the person is not merely a succession of events but a succession of crises. Crises affect us deeply and impel us to make existential choices. When we are in crisis, objectivity is ruled out.

With the intensification of subjectivity we develop an ethical outlook and we become more human. Kierkegaard sees the distortion of community life, because for him life shines when there is a perfect and individual relationship with God. This relationship is like that of God and Moses in the burning or on Mount Sinai, and God and Simeon in the temple. This relationship implies distinctiveness for different persons. But one thing is common to all, i.e. to become more subjective and more Christian and not to escape from suffering. There is no meaningless of suffering in guilt and sin, and going through them makes us more human, for religious existence is essentially suffering, and that not as a transitional moment, but as persisting. But suffering is precisely inwardness. This inwardness marks itself off from the aesthetic existence is essentially enjoyment and ethical existence struggle and victory.

An objective acceptance of Christianity is thoughtlessness or paganism. Christianity is against any form of objectivity. It only wants the individual subject to be infinitely concerned about himself. It is subjectivity alone that Christianity is concerned with and it is only in subjectivity that its truth exists, if it exists at all. Objectivity in Christianity has absolute no existence. If its truth happens to be in only a single subject, it exists in him alone. But this does not mean that other persons are precluded from the truth in their respective inwardness.

Christianity wishes to intensify passion to its highest pitch and this passion is subjectivity, that is to say it does not exist objectively. To substantiate this point further, few persons have become immortal as enthusiastic lovers and great heroes. And yet being a true lover, a hero and so forth is precisely a prerogative of subjectivity, for one simply does not become a hero or a lover objectively.

In conclusion, I wish to point out that Kierkegaard has insightfully brought alive the importance of the individual person. It was particularly meaningful in a context where, in the age of Hegel, the age of great systems and the consciousness of the absolute, the individual person had been lost. Its importance and relevance are still greater in the contemporary period where the threat of nuclear catastrophe haunts the mind of every right thinking person.

Kierkegaard's advocacy of the Socratic principle "know thyself" as "Subjectivity is truth" is meaningful as long as human beings, though the areas of stress and challenge can vary from person to person. Kierkegaard and other existentialist thinkers too uphold the metaphysics of the human person and this is highly laudable. Another suggestion of Kierkegaard which is worthy of consideration is that speculations about the ultimate questions of life have no practical outcome. Kierkegaard's philosophy is basically confessional, experimental and highly personal and not academic theology or theory. From the above discussion it is clear that the existential philosophy of Kierkegaard lays emphasis on authentic living. According to him, the individual should be able to take his own decision and create his or her own morals or values at a higher spiritual pursuit. In other words, in the pursuit of spirituality an individual may have to transcend even the common morality in certain circumstances. Authentic living consists of leading a life as per one's ethical and spiritual decision. But, it seems to me morals and values cannot be understood without reference to some criteria or standards. The reason being without criterion or standard it is likely to lead to moral subjectivism and solipsism. Further, without a moral standard or criterion or objective rule ethics and morality become directionless and difficult to distinguish from certain sophisticated superstitions and unquistioned metaphysical presupposition. So, it seems to me Soren Kierkegaard is in a loss for what is to be done. He took shelter in Christianity, particularly Christian concept of faith and God. It may be mentioned in this connection that according to the Christian concept of God, God is all pervasive and all inclusive. Therefore, ratiocination and objective logical reasoning have no place in accepting such religious faith. The logical consequence is that the ultimate and absolute unconditional faith is the only shelter. But now the question is; is this living in accordance with faith in the absolute, the authentic one? According to me, accepting God and unconditional surrender of faith cannot be said to be authentic. Once one surrenders to God and lives according to unconditional surrender, one cannot be said to live an authentic life. In this connection, it seems to me that Kierkegaard as a philosopher could not completely dissociate or detach himself from the age old belief of Christianity.

But, I do have some serious objections. Firstly, by stressing too much on individual inwardness and subjectivity, he has neglected the importance of inter-subjectivity and collective life. Secondly, if I understand him aright he stresses crucial decisions and existential choice without granting that they involve rigorous reflection. Thirdly, his concepts of sin and suffering with the help of faith do not make much sense to me. For if certain concepts are accepted by means of faith, then there is the problem of the criterion for their selection. To my mind, Kierkegaard provides no ultimate justification, since there are conflicting claims among the different religions in the sphere of faith.

Lastly, I fail to understand why one should be all the time infinitely concerned about oneself in terms of "What shall I do?" "Where shall I go" and the like. On the whole I would frankly admit that Kierkegaard's approach to life is a significant example of human's endeavour to comprehend life in general and more particularly a poignant examination of our individual life in the very process of living it.

Bibliography

Concluding and Unscientific Postcript, Soren Kierkegaard. Translated by David F. Swenson and Walter Lowrie. Princeton University Press. For American-Scandinavian Foundation, 1941. First Princeton Paperback Edition, 1968, Third Printing, 1974.

Being and Existence in Kierkegaard's Pseudonymous Works: By John W. Elrod. Princeton University Press, New Jersey, 1975.

Training in Christianity and the Deifying Discourses which 'Accompanied' It: By Soren Kierkegaard. Translated with an introduction end notes by Walter Lowrie, D.D. Princeton, Princeton University Press, First Published in Great Britain 1941. Reprinted by Offset in the United States of America, 1944, 1946, 1947, 1952, 1957, 1960, 1964.

Christian Discourses and the Lilies of the Field and the Birds of the Air and Three Discourses at the Commution of Fridays: By Soren Kierkegaard. Translated with an introduction by Walter Lowrie, D.D. Geoffrey Cumberlege, Oxford University Press, London, New York, and Toronto. Second impression 1952.

A Primer of Existentialism, M.N. Sinha, Capital Publishing House, Delhi, 1952.

An Enquiry into the Fundamentals of Existentialism, Sailesh Ranjan Bhattacharyya, Firma KLM Private Limited, Calcutta, 1979.

The Sources of Existentialism as Philosophy, Fernando R.Molina Editor. Prentice Hall, INC, Englewood, Cliffs, New Jersey, 1969.

The Existentialist Outlook, Margaret Chatterjee, Orient Longman, Delhi, 1973.

The Encyclopedia of Philosophy, Paul Edwards, Editor in Chief Volume 3. The MacMillan Company and the Free Press, New York, Collier, MacMillan Limited, London, Crowell Collier & MacMillan, INC., 1967.